GEORGIA

A Turner Educational Services, Inc. book. Based on the Portrait
of America television series created by R.E. (Ted) Turner.

Library of Congress Number: 85-12215

Library of Congress Cataloging in Publication Data

Thompson, Kathleen.
  Georgia.

  (Portrait of America)
  "A Turner book."
  Summary: Discusses the history, economy, culture,
and future of Georgia. Also includes a state
chronology, pertinent statistics, and maps.
  1. Georgia—Juvenile literature. [1. Georgia]
I. Title. II. Series: Thompson, Kathleen.
Portrait of America.
F286.3.T45   1985   975.8   85-12215

ISBN 0-8174-428-1   hardcover library binding

ISBN 0-8114-6776-7   softcover binding

Cover Photo: U.S. Fish and Wildlife Service

        6 7 8 9 0   96 95 94 93 92

★ ★ ★ ★ ★

Portrait of AMERICA

GEORGIA

Kathleen Thompson

RSVP
RAINTREE
Steck-Vaughn
P U B L I S H E R S
The Steck-Vaughn Company

Austin, Texas

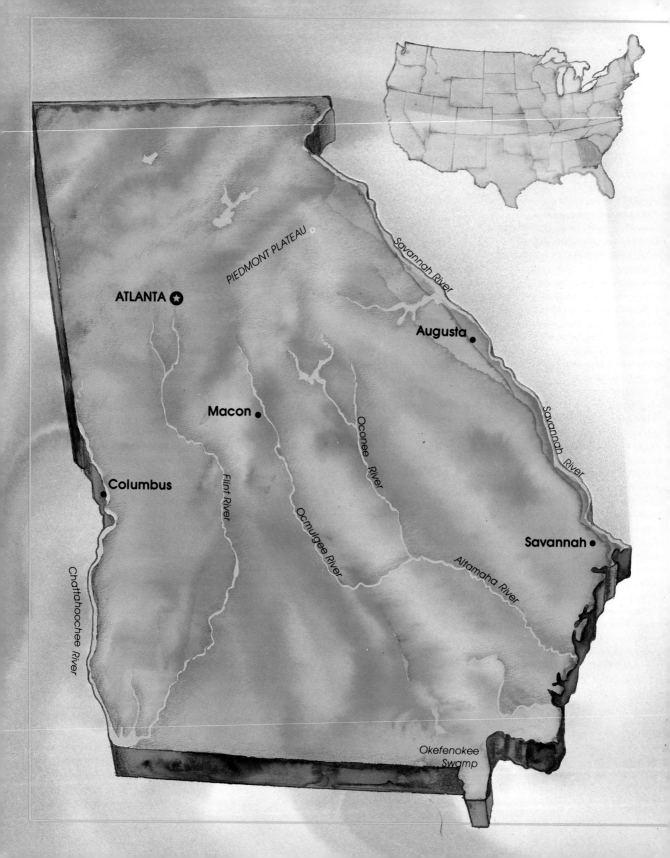

PIEDMONT PLATEAU

Savannah River

ATLANTA ★

Augusta •

Macon •

Oconee River

Columbus •

Flint River

Savannah River

Ocmulgee River

Savannah •

Altamaha River

Chattahoochee River

Okefenokee
Swamp

CONTENTS

Introduction

Georgia, the Peach State, the Empire State of the South.

"Georgia is the only place to live. These other parts of the United States and the foreign lands, they're to go and see and come back home."

Georgia: cotton, kudzu, sweet music, mills, minerals, and the Okefenokee swamp.

"You look in one direction, you might see a rolling hill. The other direction, you might see flat land. The other direction, you might see some trees or Georgia's pines."

"I say Georgia is God's country."

Georgia is lush greenery and the memory of cities burned to the ground by Union armies. It is a state drenched in sunlight and history.

Once under the thumb of King Cotton, Georgia now has thriving industry and a rich and varied agriculture. Once a slave state, Georgia became the birthplace of the modern civil rights movement.

Georgia is a state which has honored its past . . . and overcome it.

The Okefenokee Swamp.

King George,
King Cotton, Dr. King

Long before the Confederacy of the Civil War, there was another confederacy in the southeastern corner of our continent. It was a confederacy of highly civilized Indian tribes. It included the Creek and Cherokee Indians of Georgia.

Their ancestors were the Mound Builders, who had created an advanced civilization as early as A.D. 1000. Their towns were built on the same pattern as many European and early white villages. In the center was a town square or plaza with a meeting house. The individual homes surrounded the square.

The Cherokee Nation had a written alphabet, developed by a scholar named Sequoya. It had a system of courts and judges, including a supreme court.

This is a painting of Sequoya, the scholar who developed a system of writing for the Cherokee language.

9

There was nothing of the "noble savage" about the Indians in Georgia. They may have been noble. They were far from savage. They certainly dealt with the early white settlers in a very civilized way. Unfortunately, their civility was not returned.

The first Europeans to come into the area were Spanish. Explorer Hernando de Soto passed through Georgia on his way north from Florida. At the end of his journey, he discovered the Mississippi River. The area he went through he claimed for Spain.

Then, in 1565, the Spanish settled in St. Augustine, Florida, and sent missions up into Georgia. But there were no real settlements. The life of the Creek and Cherokee Indians went on undisturbed.

The beginning of the end came in 1663. In that year, Charles II of England decided to reward eight of his court favorites. He granted them the land between Virginia's southern boundary and the northern boundary of Spanish Florida.

The Spanish didn't think the land was his to give away. In their opinion, it belonged to them. But they weren't able to keep the eight men and their colonists from settling the Carolinas. Georgia became a no-man's-land in the fight between the two European powers.

So the English decided that Georgia should become their buffer zone between Florida and the Carolinas. In 1730, King George II gave the right to settle the land to a group that was dedicated to charity and reform. The group was led by General James Edward Oglethorpe.

Oglethorpe's idea was to create a colony in Georgia for people in Britain's debtors prisons. These were people who went to jail, not because they had committed crimes, but because they could not pay their bills. They would be given a choice between prison and Georgia. Other colonists would be recruited from groups who wanted to flee Europe to escape religious persecution.

Spain protested, of course. But in 1733, Oglethorpe and over 100 colonists arrived at a spot on the Savannah River. They were greeted by Tomochichi, a Creek chief whose tribe

James Oglethorpe, the leader of the first English settlers in Georgia.

lived in the area.

Tomochichi helped the colonists get settled. He also convinced the other Creek tribes nearby to allow the colonists to settle there.

In spite of the help of the Creeks, Oglethorpe's dream was not fulfilled. Few debtors came from the prisons. There were religious refugees, including German Lutherans and Mo-

11

ravians. But the Moravians were discriminated against by the other settlers because they were opposed to the war. They ended up moving to Pennsylvania where their pacifism was accepted by their Quaker neighbors.

Altogether, more than 4,000 settlers came over to Georgia in the first twenty years of the colony. Half of them came at the expense of Oglethorpe and his group. But the colony did not prosper. Oglethorpe and his group gave up their charter in 1752, one year before it would have expired.

However, settlement of Geor-

gia had begun. The foundation was laid for success in the future. And Britain's buffer zone had

The photograph at the bottom shows a plantation house (from about 1840) that was common in Georgia. The scene below is a nineteenth-century photograph of workers in a cotton field.

Georgia Historical Society

Thomas County Historical Society, Tom Hill

been established. Oglethorpe had defeated the Spanish at St. Simons Island in 1742 and pretty much put an end to the Spanish threat to English territory.

After Oglethorpe gave up his charter, Georgia became a royal colony. The farmers began to grow crops that they could sell to the English. They produced lumber, pork, and rice. They grew indigo to be used in dyeing cloth.

Georgia was the thirteenth colony. When the Revolutionary War began in 1775, it was the youngest colony, with the fewest people. It was also the farthest away from the center of colonial activity. But the thirst for independence struck quickly. The royal governor was forced to flee.

In 1776, Georgia's delegates to the Continental Congress voted for national independence. Button Gwinnett, Lyman Hall, and George Walton signed the Declaration of Independence for Georgia.

In 1778, British forces captured Savannah. In September of the next year, American forces and their French allies tried to retake the city. They were defeated and more than a thousand men were killed. The British took more of Georgia during that year but were driven out in 1782 by local patriots and units of the Continental Army.

The war ended in 1783. In 1788, Georgia became the fourth state to ratify the new Constitution of the United States.

After the war, Georgia had an enormous piece of luck. New England inventor Eli Whitney invented the cotton gin. He demonstrated it in Savannah in 1793.

Before the cotton gin, seeds had to be picked out of the fluffy white cotton bolls by hand. It was a long process. The new machine did the separating quickly and mechanically. Suddenly, cotton became a very profitable crop. Huge cotton plantations sprang up all over Georgia and most other southern states. Cotton was king.

Although the separation could now be done by machine, growing and picking the cotton still required hard manual labor and lots of it. The plantation owners bought slaves to do this work.

Land has always been the great American weakness. In every era there have been people who could not look at a large stretch of land without trying to get their hands on it, honestly or otherwise. And between Georgia and the Mississippi River, there was a large stretch of land. That piece of land inspired the Yazoo Fraud.

In 1795, a group of land companies bribed the Georgia legislature to pass a law that gave the companies ownership of more than 50,000 square miles of land at a price of less than $10 per square mile, about one and a half cents per acre! That's a lot of land and that's not much money. Because the Yazoo River ran through part of the land, the passage of the bill became known as the Yazoo Fraud.

The people of Georgia were pretty upset when they found out about the sale. They elected a new legislature that repealed the bill, but it turned out to be too late. Many of the new owners refused to give up their land. In the end, Georgia sold all its land west of the Chattahoochee River to the federal government. The

government agreed to settle the Yazoo claims.

They agreed to something else at the same time. As part of the deal, the federal government would remove all the Indians from Georgia.

It was less than a hundred years after Tomochichi and the other Creeks had welcomed

Photos by Georgia Department of Natural Resources

Europeans and given them permission to settle on Creek lands. By 1826, the Creeks had been removed to Arkansas.

It was more difficult to move the Cherokees. In some ways, they had adopted European customs and mixed them into the Cherokee civilization. The Cherokees had towns, a newspaper, a

The Cherokee Phoenix was the national newspaper of the Cherokee Nation from 1828 until 1834. These photographs show a reconstruction of the building in New Echota in which the paper was printed.

written language. When gold was discovered in the area, the Cherokees began to mine. But in 1830, Georgia passed a law saying that the Cherokees could not mine. In 1838, troops were sent in to round up all the Cherokees until they could be marched to Oklahoma. That forced march became known in our history as the *Trail of Tears*.

Seventy thousand Indians walked from eastern lands to Oklahoma. Seventeen thousand were Cherokees from Georgia. Four thousand of the Cherokees died along the way. And Oklahoma would not be the end of their journey.

Back in Georgia, cotton planters moved onto the Indian land.

At the left is a photograph of General William Sherman. The woodcut (below, right) depicts the destruction of Millen Junction, one of the places on Sherman's march to the sea.

By now, the varied economy of colonial days had disappeared. There was one crop and that crop was cotton. And raising cotton depended on slave labor.

In 1860, Abraham Lincoln was elected president of the United States. He and his party were antislavery. Southern states began to withdraw from the union. Georgia was the fifth to go.

The Civil War brought great destruction to the state of Georgia. There was a major Confederate victory at Chickamauga in 1863. But in 1864, General William T. Sherman invaded Georgia, captured Atlanta, and began his famous march to the sea.

As Sherman marched from Atlanta to Savannah, he and his troops destroyed everything in their way. Sherman reached Savannah in December. A few months later, the war was over.

After the war, the slaves were freed. There was no money to hire workers to replace them and the cotton plantations died. They were broken up into small farms that people rented and tried to squeeze a living out of. But the owners cheated the tenants and poverty became widespread. The Ku Klux Klan began to terrorize black people

all over the state and much of the rest of the south.

Georgia was readmitted to the union in 1868 and then expelled in 1869 because it would not approve the Fifteenth Amendment to the Constitution, allowing black men the right to vote. It was admitted in 1870.

Georgia was in very bad shape at this time. Its progress away from a one-crop economy was slow and often painful. By 1900, there were the beginnings of industry, which produced mostly cloth and wood products. Some farmers began to grow peaches, nuts, corn, and tobacco, but most still grew cotton. And cotton was wearing out the soil. When a plague of boll weevils destroyed cotton crops in the 1920s, Georgia hit the bottom economically.

Georgia did have a political landmark about this time. In 1922, Rebecca L. Felton became the first woman U.S. Senator.

The Great Depression of 1929 brought more hardship to Georgia. But it also brought the New Deal. Federal programs helped Georgia start on a new road.

The government gave jobs to the people of Georgia building highways, public buildings, and drainage systems. The New Deal programs also attacked soil overuse.

In 1941, Governor Eugene Talmadge got three faculty members fired from the state university system because he said they believed in racial equality. The groups which accredit universities withdrew accreditation from the Georgia state universities until 1943. Ellis Arnall was then governor and the universities were removed from political control.

Under Arnall, Georgia became the first state to give eighteen-year-olds the right to vote. And the poll tax was outlawed. Until now, the tax had kept most blacks from voting.

During World War II, defense industries came into the state. Farm workers came to the cities to take jobs in factories. The economy of Georgia was on the upswing.

The 1950s and the 1960s in Georgia were a time of tremendous activity in racial integra-

Above is Martin Luther King, Jr., standing in front of his boyhood home in Atlanta.

tion. Georgia had a very large black population and a very dark history of discrimination. Now, it became the birthplace of the Civil Rights movement. Dr. Martin Luther King, Jr., and his Southern Christian Leadership Conference led the nation towards a dream of equality.

In 1964, Leroy Johnson was elected to the Georgia senate, the first black since Reconstruction. In 1965, Julian Bond, a black civil rights leader, was elected to the Georgia House of Representatives. The other members of the House refused to let Bond take his seat. The reason they gave was that he opposed the United States involvement in Viet Nam. In 1966, the U.S. Supreme Court declared that Bond should be seated.

The last couple of decades have been a time of economic growth for Georgia. The state has continued to produce black leaders like Andrew Young, once a U.S. Congressman and later ambassador to the United Nations. In 1973, Maynard H. Jackson was elected mayor of Atlanta and became the first black mayor of a large Southern city.

It has been a long and difficult road from that first settlement at Savannah. But the people of Georgia have a great affection for their beautiful state and they can now look forward with confidence to its future.

A Time and a Place for History

"In 1951 I wouldn't even stop for gas in Georgia."

Andrew Young, former congressman from Georgia and United States ambassador to the United Nations from 1977 to 1979, knows what the south was like before the movement for civil rights. He knows what Georgia was like. And when it began to change.

"Georgia was the worst state in America. It had the most poverty. It had the most terrible racism. But I think along about 1960—well, in fact, even when I came here as a pastor in 1955— we began to deal with those problems. We began to deal with problems of race. We began to deal with problems of poverty. We took them on together. And in the process of facing head-up those kinds of difficult problems, I think we generated a new leadership that had world-wide relevance. Because every place in the world, every place, has problems of race and culture and poverty."

At the left is Andrew Young against the background of Georgia's state capitol building.

Racism is part of the dark side of Georgia's history. But the struggle to overcome discrimination has become one of Georgia's proudest moments. The black population of this state showed the way for people all over the country and the world. The strong, nonviolent protest that began here became a model in the move toward civil rights for all citizens.

"I would even say that Atlanta created the civil rights movement. It gave us Martin Luther King. It was the base of the Southern Christian Leadership Conference. The Atlanta sit-in movement was the pioneering movement which led to student movements in two hundred different cities in the nation. Almost all of the patterns that eventu-

Photos by AP/World Wide

ally worked in other places were pioneered here in Atlanta."

The dream of equality for all people has not been realized—here or anywhere. More pain will be suffered. More children will live and die in poverty. But in the last three decades, a nation has begun to come to terms with it problems. Too often we seem to speak of the unrest of the fifties and sixties, the demonstrations and the marches, as though they were the beginning of the problem. In fact, they were the beginning of the solution. It was a time when history was being made in Georgia.

"There is no city, there is no state, there is no nation that does not have problems of racial and ethnic diversity and problems between its haves and its have-nots. I don't know a state that has gone further in dealing with those problems than we have. We've still got a long way to go, but we know the problems. We know we can deal with them. And we're working on it."

These two photographs highlight Reverend Martin Luther King, Jr.—one of the most powerful forces in the Civil Rights Movement. At the left, he is shown in the late 1960s in a civil rights march. With King are the reverends Ralph Abernathy (right) and J. Ralph Jackson (left). Above, King is shown with Abernathy and Reverend Glenn Smiley.

23

The Land of Cotton

Georgia is the largest state east of the Mississippi. Once, the land here was covered with cotton plantations. The whole economy of the state depended on growing and harvesting cotton.

Today, Georgia's largest single source of income is still cotton. Now the money comes not from growing cotton, but from spinning and weaving it.

Georgia is no longer primarily an agricultural state. Manufacturing accounts for 79 percent of the value of all goods produced in the state. And the largest area of manufacturing is textiles. Mills in the state produce cotton cloth and other textiles worth about $2.5 billion each year.

Next to textiles, food processing is the most important

A modern textile mill.

Photos by Georgia Department of Industry and Trade, Tourism Division

At the far right is a Georgia peach, for which the state is famous. In the background, lumber is being prepared to go to a mill. Wood products have been produced in Georgia since colonial times.

industry. A big part of that is the processing of food grown here in Georgia. Peanut butter and peanut oil are major products. Fruit, seafoods, and vegetables are also frozen and canned in Georgia factories.

Transportation equipment, chemicals, and wood products are other important industries.

Lumber, paper, and other wood products have been produced in Georgia since its earliest days as a colony. Along with textiles, it ranks as one of the oldest industries in the state. About 70 percent of the land in Georgia is covered with forest, including the famous Georgia pine.

Clearly, most of the manufacturing in Georgia is connected to agriculture and the riches of the land.

Farming is still of great importance to the state. Today, the biggest moneymaker is not cotton, but chickens. Georgia produces about 560 million broilers

every year. It's also a leader in egg production.

As for field crops . . . well, just about anything that can be grown in this country can be grown in Georgia.

Peanuts are the biggest crop. Soybeans follow close behind. But Georgia's farmers also grow pecans, sweet potatoes, cabbage,

snap beans, corn, and tomatoes. They raise a variety of animal feeds. And they grow peaches.

One of Georgia's nicknames is the Peach State. Georgia peaches are famous. And while nobody's ever written a song about the Georgia watermelon, the state is also a leader in the production of that fruit.

The land of Georgia is not only rich. It is beautiful. Tourists from all over bring about $4 billion a year into the Georgia economy. They come to see the pre-Civil War architecture of Savannah, the Little White House near Warm Springs where President Franklin Roosevelt died, the mounds left behind by ancient Indian tribes . . . and the Okefenokee swamp.

These photographs convey some of the rich contrasts that draw tourists to Georgia . . . mountains in the northeast (left), wildlife (above, left), historic architecture (right), and beautiful coastal areas (below).

The Okefenokee Swamp

"Well, my name is Ralph Davis, and I was born and raised in the edge of the Okefenokee Swamp. I still live right where I was born—seventy-one years to be exact."

Down in southern Georgia, there is a swamp. This is not just any swamp. It is the largest freshwater basin in the United States. It's called Okefenokee.

"The swamp is forty miles wide and sixty miles long. And around the perimeter of the swamp, about every mile or mile and a half, there was a family of people that once lived around the swamp. Before the government bought it, we made a living out of it, taking people out there to fish and hunt and all these things."

Portrait of America

The swampers weren't farmers. They didn't have jobs in town, most of them. The swamp was their home and their living. They respected it in a way that harks back to a people that lived on this land centuries ago.

"It was a hard life, but it was a good life. The Okefenokee Swamp, to the swampers that lived in this swamp and around the perimeters of the swamp—

they used it like the western people and the Indians used the buffalo. If they needed something, they went into the swamp and got it. They didn't try to destroy everything. They just took what they needed."

They also respected the dangers of the swamp and the creatures that lived in it. Ralph Davis still does.

"Anything that gets in the water out there is groceries for that alligator. But when you're traveling through the swamp, there's a lot of eyes that are looking at you that you don't see."

Today, Ralph Davis spends his time greeting the visitors who come to the swamp. He's restored his homestead, and he stands on the porch welcoming folks who have come for a glimpse of an almost forgotten way of life.

"I am one of the last swampers. In fact, I am the last real swamper. I was born and raised right in the perimeter of the swamp, and I have been all over it day and night, and I know more about it than anybody living. And they ain't nobody else in the country can say that."

At the left is Ralph Davis, against the background of the Okefenokee Swamp.

31

Art Among the Kudzu

"This is a great place for poetry. You sit inside your body, you look out, you get a little crazy. . . . I mean, you sit on a porch, and it's 110, and the humidity is 90, and you start to conjure up things. It's a great place for inner worlds to emerge. There isn't enough time to hold back. The temperature won't allow it."

Some painters might prefer big artists' lofts in Greenwich Village or the Left Bank of Paris. James Herbert likes his front porch in Athens, Georgia. He likes living here. And more, he likes painting here.

"The minute you are here, you know you're not somewhere else. This is a very, very special place. I think all of the artists who work here—I don't mean just doing a barn on a hillside, I don't just mean documenting the existence around us by looking at it. I'm talking about something different. I'm talking about just the way things feel. They feel different here. It feels very old."

It's not just that Georgia is beautiful, though it is that. There are other beautiful places in the world. James Herbert has found here something like what Gauguin found in his tropical island, what Grant Wood found in Iowa, what Georgia O'Keeffe found in New Mexico. Georgia feels the way he wants to paint.

"Randall Jarrell, the poet, said that it was like the wet underside of a board, you know, this kind of crawly stuff, a little bit dark, a little bit sinister. And it really changed my painting. I started painting very shortly after I got here and the colors shifted from cool blues and cold reds into very hot, sappy yellows and reds. . . . I think that artists immediately respond to the quality of the air and the light around them. This air and light was hot, and it was warm colors, and it was thick. And my painting went right along with that exactly."

Artists work with color and light. It's not surprising that the color and light around them make a difference to them. But they probably make a difference to the rest of us, too. More than we know.

James Herbert is an internationally known painter. He's been asked to come to other places and work outside Georgia. He's been tempted.

At the right is James Herbert, with his painting "Muffin Man" in the background. Herbert is also shown (above, right) at work on a painting.

"A number of years ago, I was offered a job at the University of Illinois, and I flew out there. Going around the campus—it was just flatness. And I came back here riding the bus back into Athens, somewhere out around Toccoa —somewhere. All of a sudden the kudzu starts really burgeoning, this voluptuous stuff, green, wonderful green, bubbling everywhere and just embracing me. And I started to cry. Because I said, 'No, this is where I have to be. I gotta come back here.'"

Sweet Georgia Art

"**I** have read time in the rock and in the human heart. . ."

The words belong to Conrad Aiken, one of Georgia's two great poets. The feeling is the feeling of art in Georgia.

A sense of time is all around you in Georgia. It's time that has been filled with suffering. It's time spent with and on the land.

Conrad Aiken was a Pulitzer Prize winning poet who was born in Savannah in 1889, eight years after the death of Georgia's other fine poet, Sidney Lanier. Lanier began his short life in Macon in 1842.

Writing at a time when American literature was still young, Lanier brought to it a freshness that was rare. His poems are filled with sharply observed details and concrete

Sidney Lanier (left) is best-known for his poems about the South.

images. In words like these, we can see and feel the heart of Georgia:

I have come ere the dawn, O beloved,
my live-oaks, to hide
In your gospelling glooms,—to be
As a lover in heaven, the marsh my
marsh and the sea my sea.

Each in his or her own way, the novelists of Georgia have also explored time, the land, and the human heart.

In 1936, the huge Civil War novel, *Gone With the Wind*, was published. Its author, Margaret Mitchell had spent years of her life writing it. It became one of the most popular books of that or any other time. It has been said that Harriet Beecher Stowe's *Uncle Tom's Cabin* was the book that started the Civil War. Certainly, *Gone With the Wind* was the book that immortalized it.

Four years earlier, a book was published that showed the dark underside of life in the south. Erskine Caldwell's *Tobacco Road* was about life among the southern poor.

Carson McCullers' first novel was published in 1940. It was a sad, touching book called *The Heart Is a Lonely Hunter*. In it, a number of lonely people each find someone to talk to. Each one pours out his or her hopes, sorrows, and dreams to one man—who can neither hear nor speak.

Frank Yerby wrote many sweeping historical novels. He was one of the first blacks to become a truly popular writer.

Two short story writers must be included in the roll of Georgia writers. Joel Chandler Harris, in the second half of the nineteenth century, wrote the famous Uncle Remus stories. Flannery O'Connor, in the 1960s began to write her honest, moving, and often funny stories about everyday life, collected in books like *Everything That Rises Must Converge*.

More recently, Georgia novelist Alice Walker has won the 1983 Pulitzer Prize for her sensitive book, *The Color Purple*. And poet James Dickey writes with the richness and rhythms of Georgia's heritage.

And then there is the music.

"I have read time in the rock and in the human heart . . . "

At the right is Margaret Mitchell, with a poster for the movie version of her novel Gone With the Wind.

In new screen splendor...
The most magnificent picture ever!

DAVID O. SELZNICK'S PRODUCTION OF MARGARET MITCHELL'S

"GONE WITH THE WIND"

Winner
of Ten
Academy
Awards

STARRING
CLARK GABLE
VIVIEN LEIGH
LESLIE HOWARD OLIVIA de HAVIL

A SELZNICK INTERNATIONAL PICTURE · VICTOR FLEMING · SIDNEY HOWARD · METRO-GOLDWYN
STEREOPHONIC SOUND·METROCOLOR *

Music from the Heart of Georgia

"The church, starting in the very early beginnings of this country, was the one source of freedom, it was the one chance for the black person to express his joys or his disappointments or his hopes, his dreams, his aspirations. And hence, the music has a very emotional quality to it. To me, it is the real American music."

Phil Walden is a music producer in Macon, Georgia. Having worked with hundreds of musicians—black and white—he sees gospel music as the root of much of the popular music in this country. And a lot of that music has come from Georgia. The list of great names goes on and on.

"You can take Ray Charles, Little Richard, James Brown and Otis Redding, and it's almost impossible to measure the influence that they had and are continuing to have today on what we call contemporary pop music. It's so real and so emotional and so Georgian and so southern, what they are doing. They are products of this state's culture, of this state's heritage."

Cardell Jones of Savannah, Georgia

Portrait of America

Cardell Jones of Savannah, Georgia

The list goes on to Isaac Hayes, the Allman Brothers Band . . . there is a rich lode here that Georgia's music producers and publishers have mined. It's a Georgia tradition, according to music publisher Bill Lowry.

"We've always been involved in music in our state. Some of the first recordings ever made outside of the laboratories—at least that's what they called them back then—of the record companies were made here in Atlanta, Georgia."

Maybe it's something in the warm beauty of the state. Maybe it comes out of the history of suffering. But music—American music—seems to grow out of the Georgia soil.

"If you look at so many of them, everything from the writers to the singers to the composers—this environment, this heritage, this culture—it would be difficult to name another state that has presented the world with the amount of unusual, one-of-a-kind artists that this state can claim."

The music of Georgia also seems to take strands from all parts of the culture. It's not one kind of music, or one kind of experience. It's a blend, a cross breeding.

"Maybe that's what Georgia music is. Maybe it's made up of gospel, rock, black music, pop music, country. Maybe that's what we've really put together here in Georgia."

Georgia's music seems as if it could have come out of the beauty of the land. Two prominent figures in Georgia music are Isaac Hayes (right) and music publisher Bill Lowry (below, right).

Georgia Department of Industry and Trade, Tourism Division

The Sun Shines Bright on Georgia's Future

When you talk about the future of Georgia, it's probably good to remember Andrew Young's words.

"We've still got a long way to go, but we know the problems. We know we can deal with them. And we're working on it."

Georgia has all the advantages of a sunbelt state like Arizona or New Mexico. But they have something else that gives them an edge on the future. Many of the problems that are facing the big new cities, the utopias of high tech, are problems that Georgia has been dealing with for years. Here, they have learned some ways to solve those problems. They have gained a confidence that comes from experience. And they're working on it.

The Atlanta skyline.

Because of the contrast between its difficult past and its bright future, Georgia sometimes seems brand new. In cities like Atlanta, the young urban professionals boldly explore the new technology, the new communications networks. The sun is shining brightly on a brand new day.

But the older Georgians know that the sun makes shadows. In those shadows are overcrowded cities, poverty, discrimination, abuse of the land. These are the problems that many states face for the first time and Georgia has been working on for a hundred years.

And perhaps there's something else, something that goes with a sense of history, that gives Georgia an edge on tomorrow. President Jimmy Carter explains.

"My children will be the sixth generation on the same land. Our orientation toward the earth with the farmland and the soil has been a very great stabilizing effect in our lives. . . . And the closeness of the soil, I think, gave us attitudes that let us have faith in the future."

Georgia's history is tied to the land. That point is underlined by Georgian Jimmy Carter . . . a U.S. president whose family has lived on the same land for about 100 years.

Important Historical Events in Georgia

1540 Spanish explorer Hernando de Soto crosses through the Georgia region on his way from Florida to the Mississippi River.

1566 Pedro Menéndez de Avilés is sent by Spain to drive French settlers out of the southeast. He builds a fort on St. Catherines Island and claims the area for Spain.

1629 The English also claim the Georgia area.

1721 Fort King George is built on the Altamaha River.

1730 Plans are made by James Oglethorpe and others to create a colony in Georgia for debtors.

1732 King George II grants a twenty-one-year charter to create the Georgia colony in America for imprisoned English debtors.

1733 General James Oglethorpe arrives in Georgia with the first English settlers and founds Savannah. The Creek Indians sign a land treaty with the colonists.

1739 War breaks out between England and Spain over illegal trading and a boundary dispute between Georgia and Florida. James Oglethorpe tries to capture Florida but fails.

1740 Georgia supports the British in their fight against Spain.

1742 Oglethorpe and his troops stop the Spanish from landing in the Battle of Bloody Marsh on St. Simons Island.

1754 King George makes the Georgia colony a royal province.

1763 The Treaty of Paris extends Georgia west to the Mississippi and south to St. Marys River.

1776 The first fighting between Georgians and the British takes place in March.

1777 Georgia's first state constitution is adopted.

1778 Georgia approves the Articles of Confederation on July 24. The British capture Savannah.

1782 Americans, with the help of the French Navy, drive the British out of Georgia.

1785 The University of Georgia is created at Athens.

1786 A temporary state capital is set up at Augusta.

1788 Georgia ratifies the Constitution and enters the Union as the fourth state on January 2.

1793 Eli Whitney invents the cotton gin near Savannah.

1795 Land companies and state legislators become involved in a land fraud scandal known as the Yazoo Fraud.

1802 Georgia agrees to sell its lands west of the Chattahoochee River to the federal government. The federal government promises to settle the land claims involved in the Yazoo Fraud.

1804 The state capital is moved to Milledgeville.

1819 The first steamship to cross the Atlantic, *The Savannah*, sails from Savannah to Liverpool, England.

1827 The Creek Indians sell their lands in Georgia to the federal government and move to the Arkansas Territory.

1838 The last of the Cherokee Indians are moved by federal troops out of Georgia and onto a reservation in present-day Oklahoma. The evacuated land is quickly planted with cotton.

1861 Georgia becomes the fifth southern state to secede from the Union on January 19. Georgian Alexander H. Stephens is elected vice-president of the Confederate States of America.

1863 The Confederate Army wins its first major battle against the Union Army at Chickamauga.

1864 Union General William T. Sherman burns Atlanta and marches across Georgia to capture Savannah.

1870 Georgia is readmitted to the Union.

1922 Rebecca L. Felton becomes the first woman U.S. senator.

1945 The new state constitution is adopted.

1952 The Clark Hill Dam is finished.

1963 The first nuclear reseach center in the South is opened at the Georgia Institute of Technology.

1973 Maynard Jackson, Jr., is elected mayor of Atlanta—the first black mayor of a major southern city.

1977 Former Georgia Governor Jimmy Carter is elected the thirty-ninth president of the United States.

1983 Georgia adopts its present state constitution.

Georgia Almanac

Nickname. The Empire State of the South; The Peach State.

Capital. Atlanta.

State Bird. Brown thrasher.

State Flower. Cherokee rose.

State Tree. Live oak.

State Motto. Wisdom, Justice, and Moderation.

State Song: Georgia on My Mind.

State Abbreviations. Ga. (traditional); GA (postal).

Statehood. January 2, 1788, the 4th state.

Government. Congress: U.S. senators, 2; U.S. representatives, 10. **State Legislature:** senators, 56; representatives, 180. **Counties:** 159.

Area. 58,876 sq. mi. (152,488 sq. km.), 21st in size among the states.

Greatest Distances. Highest: Brasstown Bald Mountain, 4,784 ft. (1,458 m). **Lowest:** sea level, along the Atlantic Ocean. **Coastline:** 100 mi. (161 km.).

Population. 1980 Census: 5,464,265 (19% increase over 1970), 13th in size among the states. **Density:** 93 persons per sq. mi. (36 persons per sq. km.). **Distribution:** 62% urban, 38% rural. **1970 Census:** 4,587,930.

Economy. Agriculture: broilers, peanuts, eggs, soybeans, beef cattle, hogs. **Fishing:** shrimp, crabs. **Manufacturing:** textiles, food products, chemicals, clothing, lumber and wood products, electric machinery and equipment. **Mining:** clay, stone, sand, and gravel.

Places to Visit

Atlanta Historical Society in Atlanta.
Callaway Gardens, near Pine Mountain.
Dahlonega Gold Museum.
Etowah Mounds, near Cartersville.
Historic Savannah Waterfront District.
Lake Lanier Islands, near Buford.
Little White House in Warm Springs.
Okefenokee Swamp, southeastern Georgia.
Westville in Lumpkin.

Annual Events

Georgia Day in Savannah (February).
Masters Golf Tournament (April).
Blessing of the Shrimp Fleet in Brunswick (May).
Rabun County Mountaineer Festival in Clayton (June).
Watermelon Festival in Cordele (July).
World Championship Skeet Shoot in Savannah (August).
Fall Country Music Festival in Hiawassee (October).
Gold Rush Days in Dahlonega (September).

Georgia Counties

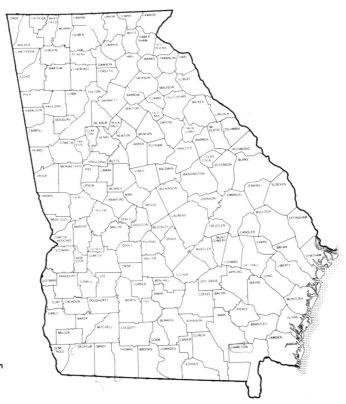

INDEX